7 Habits Why You're Still Poor

HOW TO BREAK FREE FROM THESE HABITS AND ACHIEVE FINANCIAL FREEDOM

By
Williams Chad

Table Of Contents

Copyright (©) 2023

INTRODUCTION
WHY YOU'RE STRUGGLING FINANCIALLY

There once was a man named Jack. In one of the major eateries in the city, Jack works as a chef. He earns between $1500 and $3,000 a month. He is a lone resident. He aspired to succeed in life and start his own restaurant someday. But, despite his best efforts, he constantly appeared to be having financial difficulties.

He put in a lot of time and effort at work and tried to save as much money as he could, but it never seemed to be enough. Although earning as much money as he did, he was always concerned about how he would put food on the table and pay his obligations. One day, Jack ran across an old, knowledgeable guy who questioned him about his money difficulties. The elderly guy took Jack on a journey to assist him comprehend because Jack didn't know the answer. The elderly guy pointed out all the items Jack had spent his money on as they walked across the city. Jack became aware of his large expenditures on unnecessary items. He spent a lot of money on clothes, enjoyed fine dining, and spent nearly every evening out with friends. The elderly guy said that Jack would never be able to save enough money to realize his aspirations if he kept spending his money on items he didn't need. He urged Jack to set up and adhere to a budget, to save money, and to make good investments. Although it was initially challenging for Jack to alter his spending patterns, he gradually got the hang of it. He reduced his wasteful spending and began investing and conserving money. He divides his daily paycheck into three equal portions: one for savings, one for investments, and one for important necessities like transportation, food, and utilities. Jack found himself on the road to fulfilling his aspirations as his financial condition gradually became better. Jack eventually came to the conclusion that his poor money management was the cause of his financial difficulties. He discovered that everyone can overcome financial difficulties and accomplish their goals with a little self-control and wise financial preparation.

If you find yourself struggling financially, it can be frustrating and overwhelming. It's easy to feel like you're stuck in a cycle of never-ending bills and not enough money to cover them. However, understanding why you're struggling financially can be the key to breaking free from this cycle. There could be several reasons why you're struggling financially. Financial struggles can not be attached to one thing only. The following habits could make up the reasons though not limited to; living above your means, not saving or investing, ignoring debt etc.

By understanding these common reasons for financial struggles, you can take steps to overcome them and improve your financial situation. Whether it's creating a budget, seeking financial advice, or taking steps to increase your income, the key is to take action and make a commitment to your financial well-being. Sometimes it's not all about how much you make, it's more about how much you spend and how much you save.

HABIT ONE
LIVING ABOVE YOUR MEANS

Living beyond your means is one of the primary causes of financial difficulties. You'll rapidly find yourself in debt and having trouble making ends meet if you keep making unaffordable purchases. Not investing or saving is another factor. Without a safety net, unforeseen costs might seriously damage your finances.

Living beyond your means is a frequent money issue that can result in stress, debt, and long-term financial problems. Although it may seem like you're enjoying a lavish lifestyle when you spend more than you make, the truth is that you're placing yourself in a risky financial situation that might have long-term repercussions.

The propensity to associate material items with success or pleasure is at the core of the problem. Society frequently places a premium on the most recent trends in clothing, technology, or luxury goods, causing many individuals to assume that possessing these things is a sign of success and prestige.

Nevertheless, the reality is that having a successful financial life depends more on how you handle your money than it does on what you own. Living beyond your means may give you a momentary rush of enjoyment or excitement, but it may be a hazardous trap that leaves you vulnerable to debt in the long run.

Debt is one of the biggest risks of living over your means. Spending more frequently than you make may cause you to swiftly find yourself in debt, which can be really challenging to get out of. Due to the high interest rates that may quickly become out of control, credit card debt in particular can be sneaky.

Living beyond your means can also result in a lack of savings or emergency cash, which can make it challenging to pay for unforeseen costs like medical bills, auto or house repairs. Because of the worry and anxiety this lack of financial security can cause, life may be difficult to enjoy.

What can you do, therefore, if you discover that you are living beyond your means? To start, you must examine your money objectively. In order to see your income and costs clearly, this entails developing a budget and keeping track of your spending. You must be really honest with yourself and search for places where you may save money.

You don't have to lead a life of deprivation if you cut back on your costs. Instead, it entails planning your expenditure and figuring out how to stick to your budget. For instance, you might need to cut back on eating out, traveling, or purchasing new clothing. By concentrating on what you require rather than what you desire, you'll be able to develop a budget that you can stick to over time. Avoiding living above your means also requires you to fight the impulse to keep up with the Joneses. You don't necessarily need to own the same items just because your neighbor has a new automobile or your pal has a brand purse. Keep in mind that neither your value nor your possession of luxury products defines your financial success.

You might need to look at ways to enhance your income as well. This might entail starting a side business, seeking for a better paid job, or requesting a raise at work. Increasing your salary will provide you more financial freedom and enable you to make a budget that is easier to stick to.

Finally, you must exercise patience and maintain your commitment to your financial objectives. It might be difficult to break the trend of living beyond your means, but with perseverance and self-control, you can build a life that is more stable financially and filled with fulfillment.

Living above your means is a risky financial trap with potentially serious long-term effects. You may build a more sustainable and satisfying life by being mindful with your spending, avoiding debt, and being dedicated to your financial objectives. Keep in mind that managing your money well and remaining devoted to your financial objectives are the keys to financial success, not what you possess. Spending less will help you attain long-term financial security and peace of mind.

HABIT TWO
<u>NOT SAVING OR INVESTING</u>

Long-term effects on a person's financial security might be severe if they don't invest or save. Savings refers to putting money away for future use, whereas investing is the process of placing money into things that have the potential to increase in value and produce income over time.

Due to a restricted income, living paycheck to paycheck, or just living beyond their means, people may not save money or invest (as we discussed earlier). Due to the fact that there might not be enough money left over after paying bills and other expenditures, it might be difficult to save or invest as a result.
Lack of financial literacy or personal financial understanding is another reason why people might not invest or save money. It's possible that many people lack basic financial literacy or are unsure of how to start investing and saving. People occasionally could feel overwhelmed by the complexity of financial goods and investing alternatives. An individual's financial future may suffer as a result of this. Without investing or saving, people would find it difficult to achieve their financial objectives, such as buying a home, covering their children's college costs, or setting aside money for retirement.

Furthermore, not saving or investing might increase a person's susceptibility to unanticipated financial problems. Without a financial safety net, people could be forced to borrow money or use credit cards to pay for unforeseen costs, which can result in debt and other financial difficulties.

So what can you do to begin investing and saving? Establishing a budget and keeping track of your spending is the first step. Finding areas where you may cut back and save money requires looking at your income and spending. The short-term sacrifices you may need to make, like cutting back on dining out or canceling memberships, will be worthwhile in the long run. After you've established a budget, it's time to begin saving. As a general guideline, try to set aside at least 20% of your monthly income. To make saving easier to manage, you may set up an automated transfer from your checking account to a savings account.

Also, setting up an emergency fund is crucial. You may use this separate savings account to pay for unforeseen costs like medical bills or auto maintenance. Your emergency fund should contain at least three to six months' worth of living costs.

It's crucial to have a long-term plan in place when it comes to investing. Finding assets that support your goals requires considering your objectives, risk tolerance, and ambitions. Depending on your objectives and risk tolerance, you can invest in stocks, bonds, mutual funds, real estate, or other assets. While investing, it's also crucial to have competent financial guidance. A financial adviser can assist you in determining your level of risk tolerance, building a diversified portfolio, and making any necessary investment adjustments.

Maintaining self-control and resisting the urge to splurge are important components of saving and investing. Living within your means, avoiding debt, and resisting the impulse to keep up with the Joneses are examples of how to do this.

Finally, failing to save and invest might result in serious financial issues, leaving you exposed to financial shocks and limiting your capacity to reach your long-term objectives. You may lay a solid financial foundation and safeguard your financial future by developing a budget, setting up an emergency fund, and investing in a diverse portfolio. Achieving long-term financial stability and peace of mind requires being disciplined and devoted to your goals. Keep in mind that financial success is a journey rather than a destination.

HABIT THREE
PROCRASTINATION ON FINANCIAL DECISIONS

Procrastination on Financial Decisions: Causes, Consequences, and Solutions.

The act of putting off or delaying a job or decision—often until the very last minute—is known as procrastination. Procrastination is a typical habit, but it may have serious repercussions, particularly when it comes to financial choices. When it comes to managing their finances, whether it be bill payment, budget creation, investing, or future savings, many individuals battle with procrastination.
It's critical to pinpoint the underlying reason for decision-making procrastination and take action to remedy it, such as consulting a financial advisor, establishing deadlines, or breaking down complicated decisions into smaller, more manageable chores.
We will examine the reasons why people put off making financial decisions in this article, as well as its effects, and offer some solutions to aid you stop this behavior.

Causes of Procrastination on Financial Decisions

Several underlying factors can contribute to procrastinating on financial decisions. Some of the most prevalent explanations for why people put off managing their money include the following:

Fear of Making a Bad Choice

Fear of making the wrong decision is one of the main reasons individuals put off making financial decisions. This apprehension may be caused by a lack of information or expertise in a particular financial field. For instance, you can be daunted by the complexities of investing or be unsure of how to handle your debt effectively. You can put off making any decision at all because of this dread, which can result in indecision.

Feeling Overwhelmed

Feeling overwhelmed is another typical reason people put off making financial decisions. Many individuals feel overburdened by the wealth of information and options available to them when making financial decisions, which can be a difficult and time-consuming process. In an effort to avoid making decisions while they are feeling overwhelmed, people may wait for things to go better on their own or until they have more clarity.

Lack of self-control

It might be difficult to follow a budget or savings plan when you lack self-control. This may result in excessive spending or a failure to save enough money for crucial objectives like retirement, an emergency fund, or a down payment on a house.

Financial Choices and the Effects of Procrastination

Financial decision-making procrastination can have a number of detrimental effects, such as:

Opportunities Lost

You run the risk of losing out on chances that might ultimately be advantageous to you when you put off making a financial choice. For instance, you can lose out on prospective gains if you wait too long to invest in the stock market. The same is true if you put off starting a retirement fund or investing in an internet business for too long. You're prone to dismissing any chance as a fraud or unworthy of your money. According to the saying, "the poor have remained poor because they are always terrified of losing money." As there is never a loss while taking a risk, those who do so are more receptive to chances. If you continue to pass up possibilities, you might not have enough money saved up for a comfortable retirement.

More Financial Stress

Making financial decisions later might add to your financial stress. You can worry about the possible outcomes or feel bad for not acting if you put off making a decision. In addition to other mental and emotional problems, this may cause worry and restless nights.

Financial Damage Over Time

Lastly, delaying financial decisions might cause long-term financial loss. You can get late penalties or have your credit score lowered, for instance, if you put off paying your payments. Delaying retirement savings might result in you not having enough money to support yourself in your later years. Delay might hurt you more financially the longer you wait to make a choice.

Solutions for Overcoming Procrastination on Financial Decisions

While it is not easy, it is possible to overcome procrastination when making financial decisions. The following suggestions can assist you in gaining financial control:

Knowing the underlying cause

Long-term stress and suffering can result from delaying financial decisions, as well as immediate worry. In order to take the appropriate action to combat procrastination, it is imperative to recognize its underlying cause. We will look at the various underlying reasons why people put off making financial decisions in this post, along with some advice on how to spot them.

Confront your phobias

Asking yourself these questions can help you determine whether fear is the main reason for your procrastination:

- *Will I make the wrong decision?*
- *Am I ok with the amount of information available?*

- *Do I feel like I lack knowledge or experience in this particular financial area?*
- *What if it doesn't work out for me?*

The foundation of your procrastination may be fear, if you responded "positively" to any of these questions. Take steps to overcome your fear since it might not be as scary as you think. You could find your breakthrough on the other side of fear. Overcome your fear and see the changes in your life over the coming months and years.

Do not multitask.

Projects should be broken up into manageable chunks, and each component should be completed uninterrupted from start to end. When we are almost done with a work, we are more inclined to resist interruption. Multitasking is a misconception since we only ever accomplish one thing at a time while switching between tasks in our minds. Avoid multitasking while making financial decisions; avoid becoming stuck between options, for instance, when presented with the opportunity to buy a home, start a new business, or invest in a project. Even though you might not have the resources to manage the entire project at once, you believe that if you focus only on one, you might miss out on others. In situations like this, you should consider which option is best for you right now, taking into account the available funds, the risk, and the available options. You might then decide which is ideal for you based on this information. If you attempt to pursue them all at once, you may wind up not investing in any of them and possibly losing money in the process. When your gaze is set on 10 rabbits, you end up not catching one.

HABIT FOUR
IGNORING DEBT

For many people, ignoring debt is an issue that they frequently run into, and it may have serious effects on their financial security. Money that has been borrowed and must be repaid—often with interest—is referred to as debt. Credit card debt, school loans, auto loans, and mortgages are a few examples of debt.

People may overlook their debt as a result of feeling overburdened or ashamed of their financial status. Neglecting debt can result in a cycle of late fees, interest costs, and credit score harm. This might make it more challenging for you to get credit in the future, result in higher interest rates on loans and credit cards, and cause others to start losing trust in you.
Neglecting debt can also have psychological and emotional implications. Stress, worry, and a sense of helplessness may result from it. A person's relationships, profession, and general quality of life may be impacted by this.

People should take proactive measures to manage their debt in order to prevent the harmful effects of doing nothing. This may entail developing a budget, settling debts with lenders, and enlisting the assistance of a financial adviser or credit counselor.

A crucial first step in controlling debt is developing a budget. Setting priorities for spending and keeping track of income and costs are both required. People can find areas where their spending can be cut back and commit more funds to paying off debt by making a budget.

An additional method of controlling debt is to bargain with creditors. This may entail asking for a lowered interest rate, a shorter payment schedule, or a settlement offer. If one is having trouble making payments, it's critical to let creditors know as soon as possible because doing so can help avoid late penalties and harm to one's reputation.

A credit counselor or financial advisor might be consulted for assistance. These experts may offer direction and assistance with setting a budget, communicating with creditors, and devising a strategy for paying off debt. Moreover, they can offer information and instruction on managing credit and personal finances.

In conclusion, if you disregard your debt, it might become a pain in your flesh. You shouldn't feel at ease owing someone money. You do not have to continually come up with justifications for why you are unable to pay your debt. Your justification could be reasonable to grasp, but your creditor might not give a f#ck about it. Although it could be challenging for you, keep your image intact. So when you next receive a salary, pay off your debt by going directly to your creditor. You may find it challenging since you risk going bankrupt or lacking sufficient funds. But I can promise that you'll feel a lot better and be trustworthy.

FAILING TO NETWORK AND BUILDING RELATIONSHIPS

Regrettably, many people are unaware of the value of networking and establishing connections in both their personal and professional life. People frequently disregard the advantages of having a strong network and developing meaningful relationships in favor of concentrating entirely on their own profession and personal interests. Let's now examine the negative effects of failing to network and establish connections as well as some advice on how to boost both of these aspects of your life.

Networking and Its Significance

Each sector or career should prioritize networking. With networking, people may meet new people, develop relationships, and eventually enhance their professions. This is particularly true in highly competitive sectors, where possibilities frequently come about as a result of recommendations or referrals from others. Thus, not networking might result in missed chances and restrict your career development.

Social networking is just as crucial as professional networking. We may engage with people personally through social networks and develop deep connections. Our lives may be made more enjoyable, comfier, and supportive by our relationships with friends, family, and significant others. People can experience isolation, loneliness, and unhappiness if they don't establish solid relationships.

Opportunities Lost

As was already said, not networking may result in lost chances in both the personal and professional spheres of life. Networking frequently results in job openings, promotions, and other professional improvements. These possibilities could pass you by if you don't network and cultivate relationships, which could have a bad effect on your professional trajectory.

Less Resources

With networking, one may have access to beneficial resources including career leads, mentoring, and market knowledge. Lack of relationship-building might restrict your access to these resources, which can make work success challenging.

More Stress

Lack of solid relationships can result in stress, loneliness, and emotions of loneliness. These unfavorable feelings might have a serious effect on mental health and general wellbeing. Strong connections, on the other hand, offer a safety net that can aid people in better managing their stress and overcoming obstacles in life.

Developing contacts and networking can increase job happiness. Finding purpose and fulfillment in your job may be facilitated through networking with coworkers, mentors, and other professionals in your field. On the other side, failing to network and cultivate connections might result in feelings of unhappiness and disengagement.

How to Improve Your Networking Skills

There are various things you can do to hone your abilities if you understand the value of networking but have trouble making connections:

Engage In Industry Events

Industry gatherings are excellent places to network and meet individuals in your profession. Attend trade shows, seminars, and other industry-related activities. Make an effort to make small talk and introduce yourself to people.

Social Media Usage

Networking may be facilitated effectively via social media sites like Twitter and LinkedIn. Engage with those working in your sector, pay attention to industry experts, and take part in pertinent debates.

Participate In Professional Associations

Joining a professional group may provide you access to beneficial resources, including news and events in your field, as well as opportunities to network with other professionals in your field.

Volunteer
Opportunities to network and meet new people can be found through volunteering. Search for volunteer activities that fit your skills and interests.

Attend lectures or workshops
You may meet other experts and broaden your knowledge and skill set by enrolling in seminars or workshops in your sector.

How To Develop Strong Relationships

Take into account the following advice if you have trouble creating lasting relationships:

Communication: Establishing solid connections requires effective communication. It's critical to consider the other person's viewpoint, emotions, and opinions. Between two individuals, open communication helps to build trust, respect, and understanding. Be careful to communicate in a clear, succinct manner, and refrain from being harsh or combative.

Invest quality time: It takes time and effort to create great connections. Spending time together may enrich your relationship and help you connect on a deeper level. This might be engaging in activities you both find enjoyable, having in-depth talks, or just being in each other's company.

Appreciation: Humans enjoy feeling respected and appreciated. Spend some time thanking your loved ones for their contributions to your life and acknowledging their efforts. This can take the shape of a brief thank you message or a thoughtful act like a gift or surprise note.

Be dependable: Building great connections requires being dependable and trustworthy. Be responsible for your actions, keep your word, and appear when you say you will. This promotes mutual respect and trust in the partnership.

Accept vulnerability: Being honest and upfront with your loved ones can lead to stronger bonds. This is being willing to listen to and encourage your loved ones when they share their ideas and feelings as well as being able to openly and respectfully express your own thoughts and feelings.

No one is flawless: Because no one is perfect, mistakes are bound to happen, learn to forgive. Relationships may be repaired and strengthened through forgiving one another. It entails letting go of grudges and resentments in favor of putting forward and developing as a team.

Refrain from passing judgment: Instead of being judgemental, accept people the way they are. Even if you disagree with their decisions or conduct, show support and understanding. As a result, both parties may feel comfortable being themselves in a secure and loving setting.

Respect for limits: It's crucial to respect one another's boundaries in any relationship. This entails being conscious of other people's personal space and recognizing and accepting the boundaries of what is appropriate conduct.

Be a good listener: Communication success depends on effective listening. Active listening is participating actively in the conversation, thinking about what the other person is saying, and responding in a kind and courteous manner.

Be patient: It takes time to develop good connections, so it's crucial to show patience and understanding as you work through the ups and downs of any relationship. You may create enduring bonds with the people who matter to you most if you have patience, tenacity, and a positive attitude.

To sum up, developing solid connections is crucial for leading a happy and meaningful life. You can improve your relationships and forge lifelong connections that will open up opportunities for you by engaging in effective communication, spending quality time, expressing gratitude, being dependable, embracing vulnerability, practicing forgiveness, avoiding judgment, respecting boundaries, being a good listener, and exercising patience. The secret to improving your finances is to build strong connections and relationships.

OVERLOOKING OPPORTUNITIES FOR ADDITIONAL INCOME

Many people are always looking for methods to boost their income as they deal with the hardships of daily living. But, occasionally they can be ignoring chances to earn more money that are right in front of them.

Not recognizing the worth of one's abilities and knowledge is one of the most frequent ways people miss out on chances to earn more money. Many people, for example, have valuable abilities in writing, graphic design, programming, or coaching that they may utilize to make extra money. They could, however, be unaware of the marketability of these abilities or may undervalue their worth.

Not using available resources is a further prevalent error. For instance, a lot of individuals might not be familiar with websites like Fiverr or Upwork where they can advertise their skills to a worldwide clientele. In a similar vein, they might not be utilizing social media or other online venues to advertise their abilities and offerings. By not making an investment in themselves, people also miss out on possibilities to earn more money. In order to improve their abilities and increase their marketability, this can entail enrolling in classes or earning certificates. In addition to attending conferences and activities related to their area, networking opportunities may also be considered an investment in oneself.

The sharing economy may also not be utilized by individuals. For instance, many people could have extra space they might rent out on Airbnb, a vehicle they could rent out on Turo, or goods they could sell on websites like eBay or Etsy.

Making insufficient use of tax credits and deductions is another way that people can be losing out on extra money. For instance, a lot of individuals could be entitled for tax deductions for work-related costs like home offices or other expenses they aren't aware of.
Also, individuals might not be thinking about alternate revenue sources like affiliate marketing, where they can earn commission by promoting goods and offering services. The gig economy, which allows individuals to supplement their income by doing temporary, task-based occupations, may also not be being fully utilized by the general public.

All things considered, there are a lot of chances for extra money that individuals could be missing. People may discover new methods to supplement their income and reach their financial objectives by appreciating the value of their abilities, investing in themselves, making use of the resources at their disposal, and researching other revenue sources. There are several chances available to you online in 2023. Open your eyes to them.

NEGLECTING SELF IMPROVEMENT AND EDUCATION

Neglecting education and self-improvement can have serious negative effects on a person's personal and professional lives. To be successful and competitive in today's fast-paced, constantly-changing environment, it is essential to never stop learning. This article examines the value of education and self-improvement, the dangers of putting it off, and some strategies for prioritizing personal development.

Importance OF Self-Improvement And Education

Education and self-improvement are crucial for both personal and professional development. Opening up new chances, building confidence, and improving one's general quality of life can all be a result of learning new skills, gaining information, and broadening one's perspectives. For people to remain competitive and useful in the job market, continuous learning is also essential for keeping up with emerging technology, trends, and best practices in business. Self-improvement and education also have a lot of positive effects on one's wellbeing. In order to survive in this rapidly expanding world, personal growth is very essential, especially in the domain of education. This goes beyond merely attending classes and studying. It entails using the internet to conduct research on topics you deem to be of sufficient educational depth for you. Nowadays, tens of thousands of websites are visited daily by people who live online. The internet is a key tool for enhancing your educational progress in a variety of ways. Those who put money into themselves tend to have better physical and mental health, more fulfilling relationships, and a better grasp of both their own selves and the world around them. This, in turn, can lead to a more fulfilling and satisfying life.

Risks Of Neglecting Self-Improvement And Education

There are a number of drawbacks to not placing a high priority on education and self-improvement. For instance, those who do not consistently update their knowledge and abilities may lose value and competition in the employment market. This may lead to lost chances, stagnation, and professional failures.

In addition, putting off education and self-improvement might result in boredom, irritation, and a lack of desire. People run the danger of losing engagement, feeling unsatisfied, and losing inspiration if they are not challenged or stimulated in their jobs or personal life. Burnout, depression, and other mental health problems may result from this.

Strategies For Prioritizing Self-Improvement And Education

People may, fortunately, prioritize their education and personal development using a variety of ways. Here are a few of these:

Goal-setting: Individuals may focus their efforts and monitor their progress by setting specified, measurable, attainable, relevant, and time-bound (SMART) objectives. Individuals may inspire themselves to take action and make consistent progress toward their objectives by determining what they want to do and when they want to accomplish it.

Developing a learning strategy: Individuals may maintain organization and attention by developing a learning plan that details the abilities, information, and resources required to accomplish their goals. This strategy may contain a list of books to read, classes to enroll in, mentors to find, or internet resources to investigate.

Creating time for learning: This is essential for moving forward with one's objectives. This can entail designating certain time each day or each week for learning, blocking off time on the schedule, getting up earlier or later to fit learning in, etc.

Being in a community of like-minded people: Being in a community of people who have similar interests and aspirations may be incredibly inspiring and advantageous for one's personal development. Connecting with people who can provide support, guidance, and inspiration can be facilitated by joining professional organizations, attending networking events, or taking part in online forums.

Getting a mentor or coach: Getting a mentor or coach can influence the course of your personal development. These individuals may help one manage difficulties, overcome barriers, and accomplish their goals by providing support, encouragement, and counsel. Also, they may act as a source of responsibility, ensuring that people stay on course and make continuous progress.

Accepting challenges: Accepting difficulties and venturing outside one's comfort zone can be great ways to advance and learn new things. Individuals may stretch themselves and improve their confidence, resiliency, and adaptability by taking on new work or initiatives.

CONCLUSION

HOW TO BREAK FREE FROM THESE HABITS AND ACHIEVE FINANCIAL FREEDOM

Finally, it should be noted that poverty is frequently the outcome of bad behaviors and decisions rather than exterior conditions. The reality that you might be in debt, not making enough money, living extravagantly, or not being able to save makes it difficult to achieve financial freedom. You might not have reached financial freedom yet for the factors listed above. Contrary to popular belief, becoming monetarily independent is not impossible. For one to be monetarily secure, they must be tenacious, determined, and hardworking. Your ability to make independent decisions, network, interact with wonderful people, and think for yourself is made possible by financial independence. The seven habits covered in this piece can significantly affect a person's financial condition, but they are simple to change if the necessary steps are taken.

The first habit, Living Above Your Means, is a major contributor to financial struggles. Learning to budget and prioritize expenses is crucial in avoiding this trap. Setting financial goals and creating a plan to achieve them can also help individuals manage their finances effectively.

The second habit, Not Saving or Investing, can be corrected by creating a savings plan and sticking to it. Even small amounts of savings can add up over time and create a safety net for unexpected expenses.

The third habit, Procrastinating On Financial Decision, can lead to missed opportunities, self blame and worry. Individuals should take actions and take hold of opportunities right before them. That way they are more prone to growth.

The fourth habit, Ignoring Debt, can lead to a cycle of debt and financial instability which can limit an individual's earning potential and lead to a stagnant career. Aim to pay off your debts and avoid taking on unnecessary debt. If debt is unavoidable, it is essential to create a plan to pay it off quickly.

The fifth habit, Failing To Network And Building Relationships, can lead to financial insecurity in later years. Networking with like minds is essential in creating a fast financial freedom. Like they say 'your network is your net worth'.

The sixth habit, Overlooking Opportunities For Additional Income, can prevent individuals from achieving their financial goals. Taking action and implementing the necessary changes to improve one's financial situation is crucial in achieving financial success.

The seventh habit, Neglecting Self-Improvement And Education, can lead to frustration in the near future. When you neglect certain opportunities such as getting that extra education, extra job or investing in a profitable business that could change your life, you end up staying financially stagnant.
People can take charge of their finances and escape the cycle of poverty by recognizing and changing these behaviors. It is crucial to keep in mind that achieving financial success requires tenacity, self-control, and a readiness to adapt.

Along with these routines, it's critical to develop an optimistic outlook and a healthy connection with money. One's financial position may be significantly impacted by learning to value money and to view it as an instrument for attaining financial stability and independence.

Overall, you can take charge of your finances and build a safe and prosperous financial future by avoiding these bad habits and developing an optimistic outlook. It is never too late to change, and with time, making the required improvements to one's financial position can result in a lifetime of financial success and stability. It is feasible.

Now let us wind down to some self improvement questions that could help you achieve financial freedom.

(Write down your answers in the blank space after each question)

Question One

How much do I make in a day/week/month?

Question Two

What's my debt -to-income ratio (Try not to scream)

Question Three

Am I in debt? (If not, write down where your money is going. That's what you always spend your money on)

Question Four

Who am I indebted to?

Question Five

How do I clear my debt and what plans do I have to achieving that?

Question Six

What is my daily/weekly/yearly plan towards achieving my financial goal?

Question Seven

What am I currently doing (career type) and how serious am I with life in general? (it could be that you're working or you're still a student)

Question Eight

How do I improve in my current business/workplace or school so as to stand out? This could be you learning a new skill or improving in the one you have. As a student you could learn a skill (web development, crypto trading, graphics, marketing, writing and publishing books).

Proper calculation....

To make a monthly budget, start by adding up all sources of income, including salaries, interest, pension, and spouse's income. If taxes are not automatically taken out, remember to include them as an expense. Keep track of expenses by dividing them into fixed costs, such as rent and insurance payments, and flexible expenses, such as food and entertainment. Estimate expenses that change significantly each month by using a three-month average. Subtract total expenses from total income to determine if you are spending less than you earn. If the result is negative, trim expenses to live within your means. Track income and expenses monthly to ensure you stick to your budget, and allow time to find the balance that works best for you.

Read this....

-Never be in debt and pay up if you're already in debt

-Learn something new. It could be in or outside what you are already doing (in any field you like, tech, crypto, marketing, writing etc).

-Package what you have learnt

-Sell what you have learnt. (You can reach millions of people all over the world from the comfort of your home by simply leveraging the power of the internet. Create whatever new skill you have learnt as a course, put a price tag, post on all your social media handles; e.g. Facebook, Instagram, Twitter, Tiktok and the rest. Then run ads to reach more customers) NB: Whatever you have learnt and will put out there, there are already people doing it, now look at what they are doing,then find a way to make yours unique.

-Make money

'The world is yours'.

www.ingramcontent.com/pod-product-compliance
Lightning Source LLC
Chambersburg PA
CBHW080230220526
45467CB00035B/3397